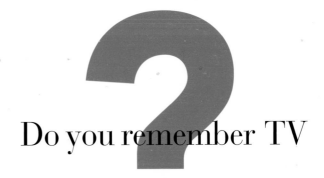

Do you remember TV

THE BOOK THAT TAKES YOU BACK

BY
MICHAEL GITTER,
SYLVIE ANAPOL
AND ERIKA GLAZER

CHRONICLE BOOKS
SAN FRANCISCO

DESIGN & ART DIRECTION:
Red Herring Design: Carol Bobolts, Deb Schuler, Adam Chiu, Adria Robbin, Kim Baskinger and Maureen Rafferty

PHOTO RESEARCH:
Stella Kramer

PHOTOGRAPHY & FOOTAGE:
CBS, Corbis, Greg Davis and Bill Morgan, *Collector's Guide to TV Toys and Memorabilia 1960s and 1970s,* The Everett Collection, Globe Photos (Jerry Yulsman, Walter Zurlinden), Andrew Goldberg, NBC, The Motion Picture and Television Photo Archive (Curt Gunther, Marv Newton, Ed Thrasher), Movie Star News, Jerry Ohlinger's Movie Materials, PhotoDisc, Michael Rubottom, UPI/Corbis-Bettmann

MANY THANKS TO:
We'd like to thank many groups of people who've inspired us, both directly and indirectly, in creating this book. **Our families**, with whom in our early lives we watched a lot of television: Michele and Julius Anapol; Paul, Marion and Rudolph Vaccari; Barbara, Richard, Lory, Kelly, David and Cindy Gitter; Hasya, Alexandra and Zachary Shabtai; Guilford, Diane, Emerson, Berta and Aaron Glazer. **Our associates at M@x Racks, teachers, friends and great fans of the book** who have given us constructive criticism, priceless assistance and the occasional bit of grief: Craig Albert, Glenn Albin, John Brancati, Susan Brustman, Mike Clifford, Howard Courtemanche, Joe Cuervo, Thom Dean, John Dyche, Michele Feeney, Clifford Finn, Shibani Gambhir, Julia Gillespie, Kara Gilmore, Scott Hankes, Glenn Hinderstein, Peter Levy, Digby Liebovitz, Gene Lisiten, Pam Manela, Astrid Martheleur, Eric Newill, Mark Pascucci, Mike Reiner, Dana Reston, Steve Robbins, Seth Rosen, Carla Ruben, Giorgio Sestu, Randi Sharinn, Angela Stevens, Judy Taylor, Joan Thiel, Jim Wayand and Pim Winter. **Our friends at Chronicle**: including our editor Sarah Malarkey, Mikyla Bruder, Brenda Tucker, Julia Flagg, Julie Chanter, Tera Killip and Caroline Herter, who greenlighted the first *Do You Remember?* — for that we will be forever grateful. We would also like to thank the loyal readers of the original *Do You Remember?*, whose response to our efforts prompted another book. And most of all to Carol Bobolts, Deb Schuler, Stella Kramer and the staff at Red Herring Design, who made this project come to life. Without them, *Do You Remember TV?* would be little more than a good idea.

This book is dedicated to Jeanine Anapol, Didier Martheleur, Elaine Benson and Erika's uncle, Maurice. We think they would have enjoyed it.

Printed in Singapore

Library of Congress Cataloging-in-Publication Data:
Gitter, Michael.
Do you remember TV? : the book that takes you back /
by Michael Gitter, Sylvie Anapol and Erika Glazer.
p. cm.
Includes index.
ISBN 0-8118-2305-9 (pbk.)
1. Television programs—United States—Miscellanea. I. Anapol, Sylvie. II. Title.
PN1992.9.G48   1999
791.45'75'0973—dc21
98-45793
CIP

Distributed in Canada by
Raincoast Books
8680 Cambie Street
Vancouver, B.C. V6P 6M9

1   2   3   4   5   6   7   8   9   10

Chronicle Books
85 Second Street
San Francisco, CA 94105
www.chroniclebooks.com

It's amazing to think that the first *Do You Remember?* has already sold more than 100,000 copies! After reading the suggestions that poured in, the ones that triggered our fondest memories pertained to television. We immediately began humming favorite theme songs and reliving episodes that made us laugh and cry.

Who doesn't know the words to the *Gilligan's Island* theme song? Many a younger sibling forgot to put the Winky Dinks' protective plastic on the front of the screen, only to find the set completely scribbled on with crayons. A treat while growing up was staying up late to watch *Love American Style, Don Kirshner's Rock Concert* or *Bonanza*. And getting up to change the channel, moving around the rabbit ears for better reception or staring mesmerized at early TVs in windows of appliance stores was part of the TV experience for so many of us.

When we thought about all this, we knew that television should be the focus of our next *Do You Remember?* book.

Like the original *Do You Remember?,* the pages here are organized randomly, as memories often are. We must give most of the credit to Carol and the staff at Red Herring Design who once again took a massive list of "stuff" and spun it into a book that is both fun to look at and exciting to pick up again and again. This was no easy task, since a book on television can be a thousand pages without even scratching the surface, but we're sure you won't be disappointed.

As always, we welcome suggestions for the next book. You can E-mail us through our Web site at www.doyouremember.com, or fax us at (212) 873-7223.

Sit back, enjoy *Do You Remember TV?...*and awaaaaaay we go!!!

Michael Sylvie and Erika

HANNA BARBERA PRESENTS

ATOM ANT

in:

MUSCLE MAGIC

HBR

HANNA
BARBERA
ORIGINAL
T.V. STARS

SONGS:

ATOM ANT
MUSCLE MAGIC
FIT AS A FIDDLE
UP AND ATOM

FEATURING SONGS BY THE
HANNA-BARBERA SINGERS

CARTOON SERIES HLP 204

Mr. Magoo
Birdman
Fractured Fairytales
Secret Squirrel
Here Comes the Grump
Top Cat
Tennessee Tuxedo
Magilla Gorilla
Underdog
Mighty Mouse
Dastardly & Muttley
Quickdraw McGraw
Ba Ba Looey
Casper, the Friendly Ghost
Huckleberry Hound
Alvin and the Chipmunks
Felix the Cat
Deputy Dawg
Precious Pup
Josie and the Pussycats

dead ant dead ant dead ant dead ant dead ant dead ant dead ant

Sneezly and Breezly
Chilly Willy
Courageous Cat
Roger Ramjet
The Jetsons
Milton the Monster
Dudley Do-Right
Rocky and Bullwinkle
Looney Tunes

ORANGES

The Bugaloos   Kimba the White Lion

The Double Deckers

The Hudson Brothers

PORANGES

The Hair Bear Bunch

The Groovie Goolies

The Wacky Races

The Fantastic Four

Yogi Bear and Boo-Boo   The Banana Splits

WHO

The Herculoids

Lippy the Lion and Hardy Har Har

Sigmund and the Sea Monsters

Shazzan!

Gumby and Pokey

Hot Wheels

The Krofft Superstar Hour

CARES!?

Isis

Hong Kong Phooey

Speed Racer

Squiddly Diddly

Color 'n Curl

"D" BATTERIES NOT INCLUDED

It's...

A Business
A Great Life
A Hit
A Living
A Man's World
A Problem
A Small World
A Wonderful World
About Time
Academic
Alec Templeton Time
Always Jan
Anybody's Guess
Fun to Know
Garry Shandling's Show
Happening
Magic
News to Me
Not Easy
Polka Time
Punky Brewster
Showtime at the Apollo
Your Bet
Your Business
Your Move

WE LIKE KIX FOR WHAT KIX HAVE GOT, MOMS LIKE KIX FOR WHAT KIX HAVE NOT...

I'M CUCKOO FOR COCOA PUFFS!

SILLY RABBIT, TRIX ARE FOR KIDS!

FOLLOW YOUR NOSE, IT ALWAYS KNOWS...

THEY'RE GRRRRRRRREAT!

HONEYCOMBS BIG, YEAH, YEAH, YEAH, THEY'RE NOT SMALL, NO, NO, NO!

SNAP, CRACKLE, POP!

THEY'RE MAGICALLY DELICIOUS

SOUL Train

It's got a good beat and it's easy to dance to, I give it a 10.

Star Search ★ Solid Gold ★ Dance Party U.S.A. ★ The Midnight Special ★ Don Kirshner's Rock Concert

Barry Manilow singing the Bandstand theme

Clearasil and Dippity-Do commercials

"Who wears short shorts?" Nair commercial   Don Cornelius

The Spotlight Dance

Jheri-Curl and Colt 45 commercials

Ob-La-Di, Ob-La-Da

a

Love and Marriage

b

STAND

c

Moon River

d

Hot in the City

e

PAINT IT BLACK

f

Reflections

g

Georgia on My Mind

h

AND SHE WAS

i

a *Life Goes On* (sung by Patti LuPone) **b** *Married...with Children* (sung by Frank Sinatra) **c** *Get a Life* (by R.E.M.) **d** *The Andy Williams Show* (by Henry Mancini and Johnny Mercer) **e** *Booker* (sung by Billy Idol) **f** *Tour of Duty* (by The Rolling Stones) **g** *China Beach* (by Diana Ross and The Supremes) **h** *Designing Women* (sung by Ray Charles) **i** *Flying Blind* (by David Byrne, sung by the Talking Heads)

flick your Bic

...this tape will self-destruct in five seconds...

MISSION: IMPOSSIBLE

"CHiPs"

ALF

WILD C.A.T.S.

H.E.L.P.

DEA

THE KIDS FROM C.A.P.E.R.

W.E.B.

M.A.S.K.

THE MAN FROM

N.O.P.D.

U.N.C.L.E.

M*A*S*H

B.A.D. Cats

F.Y.I.

S.W.A.T.

T.H.E. CAT

M.A.N.T.I.S.

O.S.S.

M.V.P.

N.Y.P.D.

R.C.M.P.

P.D.Q.

P.O.V.

U.F.O.

Q.E.D.

THE PARTRIDGE FAMILY #4
THE GHOST OF GRAVEYARD HILL

Read the exciting novel by Paul W. Fairman
See the smash Screen Gems show on ABC-TV

FIVE WITH-IT KIDS AND ONE BEAUTIFUL MOM—
PUT THEM ALL TOGETHER, AND THEY
SPELL THE HOTTEST ROCK GROUP GOING—

THE PARTRIDGE FAMILY

READ THE WILD, WILD NOVEL BY MICHAEL AVALLONE
WATCH THE SMASH-HIT SCREEN GEMS-TV
SERIES STARRING SHIRLEY JONES

20

Rock's first family
is in big-time danger!

THE PARTRIDGE FAMILY #5
TERROR BY NIGHT
by Vic Crume

Read the exciting story based on
the Screen Gems show on ABC-TV.

It's a real spook-out—when rock's coolest supergroup
invades a mansion filled with ghosts—and deadly danger!

THE PARTRIDGE FAMILY #2
THE HAUNTED HALL

Read the novel by Michael Avallone
See the hit Screen Gems-TV series starring Shirley Jones

The rock clan's future hangs in the balance
when Keith is forced to make an impossible choice

THE PARTRIDGE FAMILY #3
KEITH, THE HERO

Read the groovy novel by Michael Avallone
See the smash-hit Screen Gems series on ABC-TV

THE PARTRIDGE FAMILY #6
KEITH PARTRIDGE, MASTER SPY

Read the brand-new novel by Vance Stanton
See the smash Screen Gems show on ABC-TV

MOVIE OF THE WEEK

Ode to Billy Joe ★ **Death Be Not Proud** ★ Dawn: Portrait of a Teenage Runaway ★ Alexander: The Other Side of Dawn ★ Marriage: Year One ★ Brian's Song ★ A Brand New Life ★ **The Autobiography of Miss Jane Pittman** ★ The Execution of Private Slovik ★ Free to Be...You and Me ★ **Sara T.: Portrait of a Teenage Alcoholic** ★ The Legend of Lizzie Borden ★ **Satan's Triangle** ★ Hustling ★ **The Boy in the Plastic Bubble** ★ Sybil ★ **Helter Skelter** ★ Raid on Entebbe ★ **Little Ladies of the Night** ★ The Dark Secret of Harvest Home ★ **Please Don't Hit Me, Mom** ★ And Your Name Is Jonah ★ Friendly Fire ★ **Like Normal People** ★ Born Innocent ★ **Black Market Baby** ★ Scream, Pretty Peggy

AIRWOLF

KNIGHT RIDER

THUNDERBIRDS

THE STREETS OF SAN FRANCISCO

A-TEAM

THE FALL GUY EQUALIZER STARSKY & HUTCH THE FLYING NUN B.J. AND THE BEAR FIREBALL XL-5 THE DUKES OF HAZZARD MIAMI VICE THE BIONIC WOMAN SPENCER'S PILOTS BAA BAA BLACK SHEEP

Oh, I wish I were an Oscar Mayer wiener • That is what I'd truly like to be • 'Cause if I were an Oscar Mayer wiener • Everyone would be in love with me •

My bologna has a first name, it's O-S-C-A-R. My bologna has a second name, it's M-A-Y-E-R. I love to eat it every day and if you ask me why I'll say, 'cause Oscar Mayer has a way with B-O-L-O-G-N-A.

the red skelton show

the burns and schreiber comedy hour

the carol burnett show

the milton berle show

the soupy sales show

How sweet it is!

Sock it to me!

the jackie gleason show

the sonny and cher show

rowan and martin's laugh-in

mama's family

sid caesar's your show of shows

shields and yarnell

donny and marie

The Devil made me do it!

the captain & tennille

sha-na-na

the smothers brothers comedy hour

the redd foxx comedy hour

Solid

12
11
10
9
8
7

1

35·33·31·29·27·25
37·39·41·43·45·47·49·51·53·55·57·59·61·63·65

abc

PRO BOWLERS TOU

32

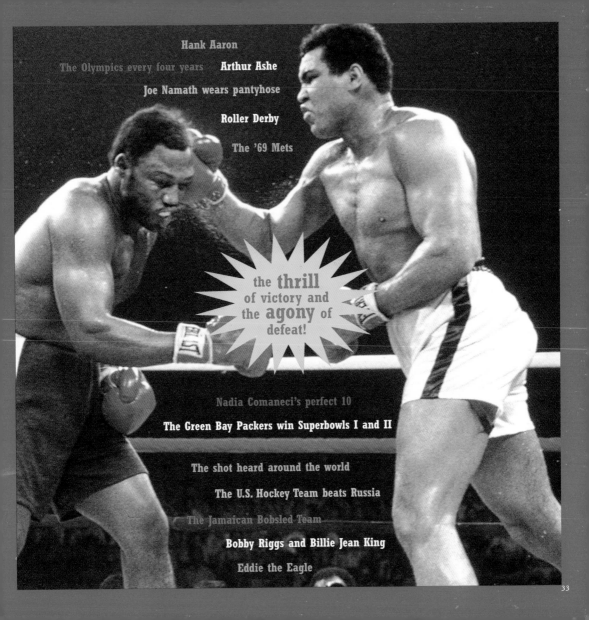

Hank Aaron

The Olympics every four years   Arthur Ashe

Joe Namath wears pantyhose

Roller Derby

The '69 Mets

the **thrill** of victory and the **agony** of defeat!

Nadia Comaneci's perfect 10

The Green Bay Packers win Superbowls I and II

The shot heard around the world

The U.S. Hockey Team beats Russia

The Jamaican Bobsled Team

Bobby Riggs and Billie Jean King

Eddie the Eagle

33

Letterman's Stupid Pet Tricks

"You like me, you really, really like me!"

Uma / Oprah

Rob Lowe and Snow White

Native American woman accepts award for Marlon Brando

Vanessa Redgrave

"Well, Ladies and Gentlemen, that was almost bound to happen. But isn't it fascinating to think that probably the only laugh that man will ever get in his life is by stripping and showing off his shortcomings." —David Niven

...and the

winner is

"Accepting the award for Woody Allen is..."

n't...

Vietnam War **Patty Hearst** Raid on Entebbe **Terrorism at the Munich Olympics** Hostages in Iran **Charles Manson** March on Washington **Love Canal** The Chicago Seven **1960 Democratic and Republican Conventions** "I am not a crook" **Apollo Missions** Martin Luther King Jr. Assassination **The Symbionese Liberation Army** The Gas Crisis **Woodstock** Son of Sam **New York Blackout**

And that's the way it is...

Elapsed Time
01:21.5

TECHNICAL DIFFICULTY

PLEASE STAND BY

There is nothing wrong with your television set. Do not attempt to adjust the picture. We are controlling transmission. If we wish to make it louder, we will bring up the volume. If we wish to make it softer, we will tune it to a whisper. We will control the horizontal. We will control the vertical. We can roll the image; make it flutter. We can change the focus to a soft blur or sharpen it to crystal clarity. For the next hour, sit quietly and we will control all that you see and hear. We repeat: There is nothing wrong with your television set. You are about to participate in a great adventure. You are about to experience the awe and mystery which reaches from the inner mind to the outer limits.

THE OUTER LIMITS

BATTLESTAR GALACTICA

LAND of the giants

CAPTAIN Z-RO

JOURNEY to the center of the earth

FLASH GORDON

ONE STEP BEYOND

THE INVADERS

space patrol

the fantastic JOURNEY

LAND OF THE LOST

SPACE: 1999

PLANET of the apes

LOGAN'S RUN

BUCK ROGERS IN THE 25TH CENTURY

The Love Boat: The Next Wave • Pacific Palisades • Sunset Beach • Malibu Shores • Savannah • 7th Heaven • Kindred: The Embraced • A Season in Purgatory • After Jimmy • Robin's Hoods • Models Inc. • Love on the Run • Burke's Law • University Hospital • Sidney Sheldon's A Stranger in the Mirror • And the Band Played On • The Heights • Melrose Place • Grass Roots • Jailbirds • Beverly Hills, 90210 • The Love Boat: A Valentine Voyage • Rich Men, Single Women • Day One • Nightingales

• Cracked Up • International Airport • Glitter • Finder of Lost Loves • Hotel • At Ease • Making of a Male Model • T.J. Hooker • Massarati and the Brain • Dynasty • Strike Force • Hart to Hart • Fantasy Island • Cruise into Terror • The Love Boat • Little Ladies of the Night • Charlie's Angels • Family • One of My Wives Is Missing • Starsky and Hutch • S.W.A.T. • Cry Panic • Death Cruise • Death Sentence • The Girl Who Came Gift-Wrapped • The Bait • The Affair • Snatched • Every Man Needs One • The Bounty Man • The Daughters of Joshua Cabe • The Rookies • The Chill Factor • If Tomorrow Comes • In Broad Daylight • A Taste of Evil • The Last Child • Five Desperate Women • The Reluctant Heroes • The Love War • Crowhaven Farm • The House That Would Not Die • How Awful About Allan • River of Gold • Run, Simon, Run • Yuma • The Ballad of Andy Crockere • The Pigeon • The Monk • Carter's Army • Honey West • Daniel Boone • The Dick Powell Show • Johnny Ringo

I TOLD TWO FRIENDS, AND THEY TOLD TWO FRIENDS, AND SO ON, AND SO ON...

You Bet Your Life / The New Bill Cosby Show / The Electric Company / The Bill Cosby

The Cosby Mysteries

Show / That Was the Week That Was

kodak

Jell-

old weird harold

I SPY

cos

"You'll never walk alone..."

MY NAME IS CHARLIE. **THEY WORK FOR ME.**

A little dab'll do ya! BRYLCREEM Ding-dong, Avon calling

Two, two, two mints in one! CERTS Cleans teeth,

CLAIROL

Something about an Aqua Velva man AQUA VELVA

Does she...or doesn't she?

FOSTER GRANT

freshens breath, naturally MILK BONE DOG BISCUITS

AVON Thanks! I needed that! MENNEN'S SKIN BRACER Kinda young,

ultra brite

Who's that behind those Foster Grants?

kinda now... CHARLIE 99 and 44/100% pure IVORY There's

51

It takes two hands to handle a Whopper

Twoallbeefpattiesspecialsaucelettucecheesepicklesonionsonasesameseedbun

You deserve a break today, so get up and get away...

Ain't no reason to go anyplace else

McDONALD'S IS YOUR KIND OF PLACE

Where's the

Big Mac, McDLT, a Quarter Pounder with some cheese, Filet-O-Fish, a hamburger, a cheeseburger, a Happy Meal, McNuggets, tasty golden French fries, regular and larger sizes, salad, chef or garden, or a Chicken Salad Oriental, Egg McMuffins, hot hot cakes, and sausage, danish, biscuits too, and for dessert hot apple pie and sundaes, three varieties, a soft serve cone, three kinds of shakes, chocolate chip cookies, and to drink, a Coca-Cola, Diet Coke, Sprite, also an orange juice. I love McDonald's, good time, great taste, and I get this all at one place. The good time, great taste of McDonald's.

Eveningwear...swimwear...

Hold the pickles, hold the lettuce, special orders don't upset us. All we ask is that you let us serve it your way. Have It your way at Burger King.

BOSOM BUDDIES

CHICO AND THE MAN

THROB

MAJOR DAD

WHAT'S HAPPENING

HELLO, LARRY

BENSON

TOO CLOSE FOR COMFORT

OPERATION PETTICOAT

JOE AND VALERIE

THE GOVERNOR AND J.J.

DOUBLE TROUBLE

THE FACTS OF LIFE

BROTHERLY LOVE

BROOKLYN BRIDGE

PICKET FENCES

COACH

BREAKING AWAY

ADAM'S RIB

WE GOT IT MADE

WKRP IN CINCINNATI

SQUARE PEGS

JORDACHE

SASSON

SERGIO VALENTE

Nothing comes between me and my Calvins

CHIC

GLORIA VANDERBILT

NO EXCUSES

Heeeeeeeee

The Mike Douglas Show

The Merv Griffin Show

The Dinah Shore Show

Dinah's Place

The Joan Rivers Show

Tomorrow with Rona Barrett and Tom Snyder

The Dick Cavett Show

David Letterman's morning show

The Steve Allen Show

Geraldo unlocks Capone's vault

Ferrwood 2-Night

The Chuck Woolery Show

The Phil Donahue Show

The Arsenio Hall Show

Open End—The David Susskind Show

The Dennis Miller Show

Into the Night starring Rick Dees

The Late Show starring Joan Rivers

The David Frost Show

The Tom Kennedy Show

Charles Perez

ere's

Floyd R. Turbo: American • Ed Ames's tomahawk throw • Broadcasting from New York • Skitch Henderson • Jimmy Stewart's poems • Ed McMahon • Joan Rivers • Tiny Tim's wedding • Lennon & McCartney • Doc Severinsen • May 21, 1992 with Bette Midler and Robin Williams

Wunnerful, wunnerful!

The lovely Anaconnie

The Lennon Sisters

Bobby & Cissy

Guy & Ralna

Myron Floren

Champagne music

Norma Zimmer

One of these things is not like the others, one of these things is not the same. Can you guess which thing is not like the others? Now it's time to p our game, time play our game.

3 FOR THE MONEY

THE THREE STOOGES

WHAT'S BEHIND DOOR NUMBER THREE

BROUGHT TO YOU BY THE NUMBER

WHEN THERE WERE ONLY THREE MAJOR NETWORKS

MY THREE SONS

3-2-1 CONTACT

THREE'S A CROWD

THREE FOR THE ROAD

THE THREE MUSKETEERS

THREE ON A MATCH

THREE'S COMPANY

3 GIRLS 3

Where, oh where are you tonight? Why did you leave me here all alone? I searched the world over and I thought I'd found true love, but you met another and PTHHP! you was gone....

Come listen to a story 'bout a man named Jed
A poor mountaineer, barely kept his family fed
Then one day he was shootin' at some food
And up through the ground came a-bubblin' crude.
Oil that is. Black gold. Texas tea.
Well, the first thing you know old Jed's a millionaire
The kinfolks said, "Jed, move away from there"
Said, "California is the place you oughta be"
So they loaded up the truck and moved to Beverly.
Hills that is. Swimmin' pools. Movie stars.

The Beverly Hillbillies

Well, now it's time to say goodbye to Jed and all his kin
They would like to thank you for kindly stoppin' in
You're all invited back next week to this locality
To have a heapin' helpin' of their hospitality

Green Acres is the place to be
Farm livin' is the life for me.
Land spreadin' out so far and wide,
Keep Manhattan, just give me that countryside.
New York is where I'd rather stay
I get allergic smelling hay.
I just adore a penthouse view.
Darling, I love you but give me Park Avenue.
The chores!
The stores!
Fresh air!
Times Square!
You are my wife!
Good-bye, city life!
Green Acres we are there.

Come ride the little train that is rollin' down the tracks at the junction,

Petticoat Junction

Forget about your cares, it is time to relax at the junction,
Petticoat Junction
Lotsa curves, you bet, even more when you get to the junction,
Petticoat Junction
There's a little hotel called the Shady Rest, at the junction,
Petticoat Junction
It is run by Kate, come and be her guest at the junction,
Petticoat Junction
And that's uncle Joe.
He's a-movin' kinda slow at the junction,
Petticoat Junction!

Billy ↑

←

↓ **The Golden Palace**

 →

↓

Diagnosis Murder ↑

↑ **Spenser: for Hire**

 →

67

	BOB & CAROL & TED & ALICE	DECEMBER BRIDE
	S.W.A.T.	PETE AND GLADYS
	SOAP	THE RICHARD BOONE SHOW
THE JOEY BISHOP SHOW	TABITHA	KENTUCKY JONES
MY FAVORITE MARTIAN	VEGA$	DRAGNET
THE COURTSHIP OF EDDIE'S FATHER	GAVILAN	DRAGNET '67
	SPENSER: FOR HIRE	THE D.A.
THE MAGICIAN	AMERICAN DREAMER	HEC RAMSEY
MASQUERADE PARTY	CROSSROADS	M*A*S*H
THE INCREDIBLE HULK	IT HAD TO BE YOU	AFTER M*A*S*H
THE BOOK OF LISTS	THE LAZARUS MAN	BLACKE'S MAGIC
	VITAL SIGNS	YOU CAN'T TAKE IT WITH YOU
GOODNIGHT, BEANTOWN	THE LOVE BOAT: THE NEXT WAVE	3RD ROCK FROM THE SUN

This is the city. Los Angeles, California. The story that you are about to see is true. The names have been changed to protect the innocent...

MIAMI
VICE •
BARNABY
JONES •
THE MOD
SQUAD •
MANNIX •
THE GIRL
FROM
U.N.C.L.E.
• IT TAKES A
THIEF • THE
ROCKFORD FILES • PETER GUNN • DRAGNET • COLUMBO • MCCLOUD
• BARNEY MILLER • POLICE STORY • VEGA$ • HONEY WEST •
MAGNUM, P.I. • IRONSIDES • KOJAK • MAYBERRY, R.F.D. •
THE STREETS OF SAN FRANCISCO • T.J. HOOKER
• SIMON & SIMON • ADAM-12 • THE AVENGERS • MACMILLAN
& WIFE • FISH • REMINGTON STEELE • MOONLIGHTING • HILL
STREET BLUES • HIGHWAY PATROL • THE HARDY BOYS/NANCY DREW
MYSTERIES • COP ROCK • THE F.B.I. • BANACEK • BARETTA • MIKE
HAMMER • POLICE WOMAN • CAR 54, WHERE ARE YOU? • CHIPS •
S.W.A.T. • HAWAII FIVE-0 •
ELLERY QUEEN
CANNON •
DEVLIN •
CRIME
STORY •
MATLOCK
• THE DETECTIVES •
EYE TO EYE • SECRET AGENT •
RIPTIDE • PETROCELLI • THE OUT-
SIDER • ONE WEST WAIKIKI •
O.S.S.

HART TO
HART • ROUTE 66 •
HAWAIIAN EYE • THE FALL GUY
• THE UNTOUCHABLES
• THE PRISONER • I SPY
• CODENAME: FOXFIRE •

THE NEW
BREED • NAKED
CITY • THE MOST DEADLY
GAME • MOST WANTED
• MATT HELM •
STARSKY & HUTCH • 77 SUNSET STRIP •
• KATE LOVES A MYSTERY •
PERRY MASON • JAKE
& THE FAT-
MAN

It's 10 p.m.

Candid Camera	The Rogues	My Three Sons	Serpico	Tucker's Witch
Loretta Young	Slattery's People	The Man and the City	Most Wanted	The Quest
Hennesey	The Doctors and the Nurses	Night Gallery	Rafferty	Remington Steele
The Barbara Stanwyck Show	The Jimmy Dean Show	Owen Marshall:	Lou Grant	The Devlin Connection
One Step Beyond	The Defenders	Counselor at Law	Baretta	Emerald Point N.A.S.
The Garry Moore Show	The Reporter	The Persuaders	Big Hawaii	Bay City Blues
Naked City	The Wackiest Ship	The New Bill Cosby Show	The Redd Foxx Comedy Hour	Hotel
Armstrong Circle Theater	in the Army	NBC Reports	Barnaby Jones	Matt Houston
The U.S. Steel Hour	The Steve Lawrence Show	America	Rosetti and Ryan	For Love and Honor
Peter Loves Mary	Run for Your Life	The Julie Andrews Hour	Quincy	The Yellow Rose
Person to Person	CBS Reports	Cannon	The Love Boat	Jessie
You Bet Your Life	Amos Burke, Secret Agent	Search	Kaz	Miami Vice
The Detectives	I Spy	Banyon	Lifeline	Finder of Lost Loves
The Twilight Zone	The Long Hot Summer	The Sixth Sense	Vega$	Cover Up
Michael Shayne	The Dean Martin Show	Medical Center	W.E.B.	Hot Pursuit
The Fight of the Week	The Man from U.N.C.L.E.	Police Story	Flying High	Our Family Honor
Gunsmoke	The Big Valley	Doc Elliot	The Eddie Capra Mysteries	The Equalizer
Adventures in Paradise	Jean Arthur	Kojak	Fantasy Island	Spenser: For Hire
The DuPont Show of the Week	ABC Stage '67	Love Story	Dallas	Hunter
Ben Casey	Hawk	The Streets of San Francisco	Sword of Justice	Jack and Mike
Thriller	Twelve O'Clock High	NBC Follies	Trapper John, M.D.	1986
Alcoa Premiere	Laredo	Griff	Prime Time Sunday	Kay O'Brien
Cain's Hundred	Mission: Impossible	Barnaby Jones	The Lazarus Syndrome	Starman
Bob Newhart	The High Chaparral	Get Christie Love!	The Best of Saturday	L.A. Law
The Untouchables	The Carol Burnett Show	The Manhunter	Night Live	Buck James
CBS Reports	The Hollywood Palace	Petrocelli	20/20	Thirtysomething
Sing Along with Mitch	Dundee and the Culhane	Harry O	Kate Loves a Mystery	The Law & Harry McGraw
Target: The Corruptors	Good Company	Movin' On	Eischied	Crime Story
Voice of Firestone	Judd for the Defense	The Night Stalker	Hart to Hart	Private Eye
The New Loretta Young Show	Mannix	Police Woman	Paris	West 57th
David Brinkley's Journal	The Beautiful	Nakia	A Man Called Sloane	Duet
The Eleventh Hour	Phyllis Diller Show	Bronk	Flamingo Road	Almost Grown
Alfred Hitchcock	That's Life	Beacon Hill	Knots Landing	Midnight Caller
The Andy Williams Show	60 Minutes	Joe Forrester	NBC Magazine	China Beach

Do you know where your children are?

The Jack Paar Program	The Jonathan Winters Show	Starsky and Hutch	Secrets of Midland Hts.	Wiseguy
100 Grand	The Outsider	Kate McShane	Hill Street Blues	Tattinger's
Breaking Point	Star Trek	Medical Story	Dynasty	Heartbeat
East Side, West Side	The Bold Ones	Matt Helm	Shannon	Tracey Ullman
The Fugitive	Love, American Style	Delvecchio	Jessica Novak	Designing Women
The Bell Telephone Hour	Marcus Welby, M.D.	Executive Suite	Strike Force	Island Son
Channing	Hawaii Five-O	Family	Falcon Crest	Quantum Leap
The Danny Kaye Show	Then Came Bronson	Switch	Cassie & Co.	Prime Time Live
Sid Caesar	It Takes a Thief	Charlie's Angels	Fitz & Bones	Saturday Night with
Here's Edie	Jimmy Durante Presents	The Blue Knight	Television: Inside and Out	Connie Chung
The Nurses	The Lennon Sisters Hour	The Quest	Cagney & Lacey	Mancuso F.B.I.
Kraft Suspense Theatre	Bracken's World	Van Dyke and Company	St. Elsewhere	Comic Strip Live

wonde

kukla, fran and ollie

winky dinks

sesame street

captain kangaroo

the billy barty show

the mickey mouse club

zoom

winchell mahoney and knucklehead

romper room

crama

the electric company

sheriff john

shari lewis and lambchop

howdy doody

Howard Borden THE BOB NEWHART SHOW

Stanley & Helen Roper THREE'S COMPANY

Steve & Marcy Rhodes MARRIED...WITH CHILDREN

Fred & Ethel Mertz I LOVE LUCY

Lenny Kowznovski & Andrew "Squiggy" Squigman LAVERNE AND SHIRLEY

George & Louise Jefferson ALL IN THE FAMILY

Tom & Helen Willis THE JEFFERSONS

Milburn & Margaret Drysdale THE BEVERLY HILLBILLIES

Ricky Segall THE PARTRIDGE FAMILY

Barney & Betty Rubble THE FLINTSTONES

Cecily & Gwendolyn Pigeon THE ODD COUPLE

Abner & Gladys Kravitz BEWITCHED

Ron & Ramona Luchesse THE DAYS AND NIGHTS OF MOLLY DODD

Jerry & Millie Helper THE DICK VAN DYKE SHOW

Irwin "Skippy" Handleman FAMILY TIES

Lars & Phyllis Lindstrom THE MARY TYLER MOORE SHOW

Ginny Wrobliki ONE DAY AT A TIME

Ed & Trixie Norton THE HONEYMOONERS

Roger & Kay Addison MR. ED

GR 5-5099 The Hogans: 555-4656 The Daily Planet: ME 6-0500 The Lawrences: 555-2134 The Ricardos: MU 5-9975 The Mertzes: CL 2-0799 The Stephenses:

One ringy-dingy...Two ringy-dingys...Three ringy-dingys...is this the party to whom I am speaking?

The Beaver, 211 Pine Street, Mayfield The Munsters,
1313 Mockingbird Lane Archie and Edith, 704 Hauser Street,
Queens Mr. Kotter, 711 E. Ocean Parkway PLEASE FORWARD 1962 Linden Blvd.
Alice Kramden, 358 Chauncey Street, Brooklyn
Felix Unger & Oscar Madison, 1049 Park Avenue, New York ANN MARIE
344 W. 78TH ST. #4D PLEASE FORWARD 627 E. 54th Street Danny, Williams,
505 E. 56th Street, NY The Andersons, 607 S. Maple Street, Springfield
Rhoda Brwwxd Morganstern PLEASE FORWARD 332 West 46th Street, NYC
Mr. Jethro Bodine, 518 Crestview Drive, Beverly Hills, CA Patty
& Cathy Lane, 8 Remsen Drive, Brooklyn Heights, NY
Dennis Mitchell, 627 Elm Street, Hillsdale Ricky, Ricardo 623 E. 68th St. #4a, NY

checking in

the jeffersons maude gloria archie bunker's place **704** hauser

good times

My name is Rhoda Morganstern. I was born in the Bronx, New York, in December 1941. I've always felt

responsible for World War II. The first thing that I remember liking that liked me back was food. I'm a high

school graduate. I went to art school. I decided to move out of the house when I was twenty-four. My mother

still considers this the day I ran away from home. Eventually, I ran to Minneapolis, where it's cold and I

figured I would keep better, and now I'm back in Manhattan. New York, this is your last chance.

UP YOUR
NOSE WITH
A RUBER
-HOSE!

I'd walk a mile for a Camel.

Just what the doctor ordered.

Winston tastes good,
like a cigarette should.

You've come a long way, baby!

I'd rather fight than switch.

More doctors smoke Camels
than any other cigarette!

Tareyton tastes better, charcoal is why.

You can take Salem out of the
country, but you can't take the
country out of Salem.

I'm not a doctor, but I play one on T.V.

87

The Alternative Factor ☆
The Galileo Seven ☆
Parts I and II ☆
Mudd's Women ☆
Where No Man Has Gone Before ☆
The Corbomite Maneuver
What Are Little Girls Made Of? ☆
Charlie X ☆ Balance Of Terror ☆
The Man Trap ☆ The Enemy Within
Tomorrow Is Yesterday ☆ Shore Leave ☆ Court Martial ☆
The Naked Time ☆
The Enemy Within
The Cage
A Taste Of Armageddon ☆ Miri ☆
The Menagerie
The Squire Of Gothos ☆ Arena ☆
The Devil In The Dark ☆ Errand Of Mercy ☆ Space Seed ☆
The Return Of The Archons ☆ The Conscience Of The King
This Side Of Paradise ☆
The City On The Edge Of Forever
Operation Annihilate
Dagger Of The Mind

88

LOST iN SPaCE

DANGER! DANGER! WILL ROBINSON...

VIDEO KILLED THE RADIO STAR

Sing Along

On your mark, get set, and go now, got a dream and we just know how, we're gonna make that dream come true—and we'll do it our way, yes, our way...make all our dreams come true for me and you...LAVERNE AND SHIRLEY She's mine alone but luckily for you, if you find a girl to love, only one girl to love, then she'll be that girl, too...THAT GIRL He protects and he saves his friends under the sea, that's where you'll find...DIVER DAN ...still they're cousins, identical cousins, and you'll find they laugh alike, they walk alike, at times they even talk alike; you can lose your mind when cousins are two of a kind...THE PATTY DUKE SHOW Tra-la-la, la-la-la, tra-la-la, la-la-la...THE BANANA SPLITS ADVENTURE HOUR

with Mitch

Phoebe Figalilly is a silly name and so many silly things keep happening; what is this magic thing about Nanny, is it love or is it magic?...NANNY AND THE PROFESSOR ...she's my very own guiding star, a 1928 Porter, that's my mother dear. She helps me through everything I do and I'm so glad she's here...MY MOTHER THE CAR ...we've got a gorilla for sale...full of charm and appeal; handsome, elegant, intelligent, sweet; he's really ideal...THE MAGILLA GORILLA SHOW ...whatever will be, will be; the future's not ours to see, que séra, séra...THE DORIS DAY SHOW ...wants a gal who's dreamy...wants a gal who's creamy...wants a gal to call his own... DOBIE GILLIS Love is crazy, it's unwise, it can take you by surprise...BRIDGET LOVES BERNIE

The Homecoming

The King
Family

The Little
Drummer
Boy

Frosty
the
Snowman

Bob Hope

The Night
Before
Christmas

The Yule
Log

"I want
to be a
dentist!"

It's a
Wonderful
Life

A
Charlie
Brown
Christmas

An American
Christmas
Carol

Dick
Clark's
New
Year's
Rockin'
Eve

Bing
Crosby

Guy
Lombardo
playing
"Auld Lang
Syne" on
New Year's
Eve

Miracle on
34th Street

DINO

ASTRO

RIN-TIN-TIN

LADADOG

TRAMP

BUCK

BENJI

TIGER

DREYFUS

EDDIE

BANDIT

PETEY

dino > the flintstones astro > the jetsons eddie > frasier tramp > my three sons benji > petticoat junction buck > married...with children dreyfus > empty nest bandit > johnny quest petey > the little rascals tiger > the brady bunch ladadog > please, don't eat the daisies

Seven Brides for Seven Brothers

Davy Crockett

The High Chaparral

Death Valley Days

The Lone Ranger

GUNSMOKE

THE BIG VALLEY

Alias Smith and Jones

RAWHIDE

"DANIEL BOONE WAS A MAN, A BIG MAN…"

HERE COME THE BRIDES

THE RIFLEMAN

Wagon Train

How The West Was Won

F-TROOP

THE WILD WILD WEST

Midnight Caller

Scarecrow and Mrs. King

M Squad

The Man from Interpol

The Ghost and Mrs. Muir

THE SAINT

The Avengers

KNOTS LANDING FALCON CREST HOTEL

PEYTON PLACE DYNASTY THE COLBYS

TV GUIDE

WITH SELECTED CABLE / PAY LISTINGS

50¢ Local Programs ◁⑴
March 27–April 2, 1982

J.R.'s Revenge
'DALLAS'—MY WAY
By Larry Hagman
Page 2

RICH MAN, POOR MAN MASTER OF THE GAME

BEVERLY HILLS 90210 MODELS INC.

Just sit right back and

from this tropic port aboard this tiny ship

Flipper

"You sank my battleship!"

sailing man, the skipper brave and sure. Five passengers

The weather started getting rough,

The Aquanauts

the tiny ship was tossed. If

Sea Hunt

would be lost (the Minnow would be lost). The ship's aground on the

with Gilligan, the Skipper, too, the millionaire

you'll hear a tale, a tale of a fateful trip that started

The Undersea World of Jacques Cousteau

The mate was a mighty

Baywatch

set sail that day for a three-hour tour (a three-hour tour).

Ask any mermaid
you happen to see—
What's the best tuna?
Chicken of the Sea!

not for the courage of the fearless crew, the Minnow

Sorry, Charlie!

shore of this uncharted desert isle,

and his wife, the movie star, the professor and MaryAnn,

here on Gilligan's Isle.

Don Adams • Edie Adams • Marla Adams • Mason Adams • Charlie Aiken • Edward Albert • Robert Alda • Norman Alden • Kyle Aletter • Debbie Allen • Jayne Meadows Allen • Steve Allen • June Allyson • Don Ameche • Morey Amsterdam • Barbara Anderson • Daryl Anderson • Loni Anderson • Melissa Sue Anderson • Richard Dean Anderson • Richard Anderson • Anthony Andrews • Adam Arkin • Allison Arngrim • Pedro Armendariz Jr. • Bess Armstrong • John Astin • Frankie Avalon • Lois Areno • Desi Arnaz Jr. • Jean Pierre Aumont • Lew Ayres • Catherine Bach • Jim Backus • Vince Baggetta • Kay Ballard • Conrad Bain • Pearl Bailey • Scott Baio • Jack Bannon • Adrienne Barbeau • Cyb Barnstable • Trish Barnstable • Gene Barry • Bill Barty • Dick Bakalyan • Diane Baker • Priscilla Barnes • Doug Barr • Richard Basehart • Kathy Bates • Anne Baxter • Meredith Baxter • Orson Bean • Beene Geoffrey • Ralph Bellamy • Dirk Benedict • Brenda Benet • Lucile Benson • Barbi Benton • Polly Bergen • Lee Bergere • Milton Berle • Warren Berlinger • Jack Bernardi • Ken Berry • Noah Berry Jr. • David Birney • Bill Bixby • Vivian Blaine • Linda Blair • Amanda Blake • Ronee Blakely • Susan Blanchard • Joan Blondell • Lloyd Bochner • Ray Bolger • Frank Bonner • Sonny Bono • Sorrell Booke • Linwood Boomer • Hank Brandt • Bart Braverman • Larry Breeding • Dori Brenner • Lloyd Bridges • Todd Bridges • Melendy Britt • Morgan Brittany • James Broderick • Philip Brown • Woody Brown • Kathie Brown • Ellen Bry • Ray Bucktenika • Bary Burghoff • Paul Burke • Raymond Burr • Dean Butler • Red Buttons • Ruth Buzzi • Edd Byrnes • Sid Caesar • Michael Callan • Charlie Callas • Catherine Campbell • Cab Calloway • Diana Canova • Judy Canova • Diahann Carroll • Victoria Carroll • Jack Carter • Peggy Cass • David Cassidy • Joanna Cassidy • Carol Channing • Cyd Charisse • Chaos • Charo • Sam Chew • William Christopher • Jan Clayton • Debra Clinger • James Coco • Peter Coffield • Dennis Cole • Raymond Cole • Dabney Coleman • Gary Collins • Cissy Colpitts • Gary Coneay • Mike Connors • Hans Conreid • Frank Converse • Bert Convy • Jeff Cooper • Alex Cord • Al Corley • Lydia Cornell • Joseph Cotten • Pat Cowley • Bob Crane • Linda Cristal • Cathy Lee Crosby • Mary Crosby • Norm Crosby • Murphy Cross • Scatman Crothers • Patricia Crowley • Pat Crowley • Billy Crystal • Robert Culp • Jane Curtin • Jamie Lee Curtis • Jon Cyphers • Arlene Dahl • Bill Daily • Jimmy Daio • Dallas Cowboy Cheerleaders • Cathryn Damon • Cesare Danoval • Kim Darby • Jennifer Darling • James Darren • Ann B. Davis • Billy Davis Jr. • Clifton Davis • Phyllis Davis • Richard Dawson • Laraine Day • Rosemary DeCamp • Olivia De Havilland • Sandra Dee • Don Defore • Bob Denver • Joyce Dewitt • Dena Dietrich • Phyllis Diller • Donna Dixon • Elinor Donahue • Troy Donahue • David Doyle • Denise Dubary • Ja'Net Dubois • Patrick Duffy • Patty Duke • Sandy Duncan • Nancy Dussault • Patty Dworkin • Leslie Easterbrook • Herb Edelman • Samantha Eggar • Robin Eisenman • Britt Eckland • Elizabeth the Koala • Ron Ely • Georgia Engel • Erik Estrada • Linda Evans • Maurice Evans • Shelley Fabares • Fabian • Nanette Fabray • Douglas Fairbanks Jr. • Morgan Fairchild • Lola Falana • Antonio Fargas • Jamie Farr • Brian Farrel • Alice Faye • Corey Feldman • Tovah Feldshuh • Norman Fell • Christina Farrare • Conchata Ferrell • Jose Ferrer • Irena Ferris • Fannie Flag • Rhonda Fleming • Charles Frank • Gary Frank • Bonnie Franklin • Pamela Franklin • Char Fontane • Phil Foster • Bernard Fox • Robert Fuller • Annette Funicello • Eva Gabor • Zsa Zsa Gabor • John Gabriel • Betty Garrett • Dick Gautier • John Gavin • Janet Gaynor • Will Geer • Christopher George • Lynda Day George • Maria Gibbs • Melissa Gilbert • Jack Gildord • Richard Gilliland • Lillian Gish • George Gobel • Arthur Godfrey • Arlene Golonka • Ruth Gordon • Grant Goodeve • Lynda Goodfriend • Dody Goodman • Michael Goodwin • Harold Gould • Robert Goulet • Virginia Graham • Fred Grandy • Farley Granger • Karen Grassle • Peter Graves • Lorne Greene • Shecky Greene • James Gregory • Pamela Grier • Rosey Grier • Tammy Grimes • David Groh • Robert Guillaume • Shelley Hack • Joan Hacket • Buddy Hackett • Pat Haden • Jackie Earle Haley • Monty Hall • Tom Hallick • Alan Hale • Brett Halsey • Halston • Nicholas Hammond • Tom Hanks • Ty Hardin • Mark Harmon • Pat Harrington • Jo Anne Harris • Phil Harris • Jenilee Harrison • Lisa Hartman • Peter Haskell • David Hasselhoff • David Hedison • Robert Hegyes • Susan Helfond • Katherine Helmond • Shirley Hemphill • Sherman Hemsley • Florence Henderson • John Hillerman • Kim Holland • Celeste Holm • Telma Hopkins • Susan Howard • Beth Howland • The Hudson Brothers • Gale Hunnicutt • Tab Hunter • Gunilla Hutton • Marty Ingels • Peter Isacksen • Reggie Jackson • Rachel Jacobs • John James • Mark James • Joyce Jameson • Conrad Janis • Maren Jensen • Arte Johnson • Bayn Johnson • Jay Johnson • Van Johnson • Carolyn Jones • Henry Jones • Jack Jones • Elaine Joyce • Ann Julian • Gordon Jump • Shelley Juttner • Steve Kanaly • Caren Kayes • Howard Keel • Stephen Keep • Patsy Kelly • Rozz Kelly • Graham Kennedy • Jayne Kennedy • Ken Kercheval • Joanna Kerns • Brian Kerwin • Meegan King • Werner Klemperer • Richard Kline • Patricia Klous • Ted Knight • Don Knotts • Koock Guich • Bernie Koppell • Nancy Kulp • Laborteaux • Diane Ladd • Judy Landers • David Landsberg • Sue Ane Langdon • Hope Lange • Kim Lankford • Fernando Lamas • Lorenzo Lamas • Dorothy Lamour • Zane Lasky • Margaret Laurence • Marie Laurin • John-Philip Law • Peter Lawford • Carol Lawrence • Tracy Lawrence • Vicki Lawrence • Brianne Leary • Michele Lee • Janet Leigh • Sheila Lenham • Harvey Lembeck • Michael Lembeck • Audra Lindley • Larry Linville • Cleavon Little • Rich Little • Tina Louise • Shelley Long • Dorian Lopinto • Joan Loring • Allen Ludden • Carol Lynley • James MacArthur • Philip Charles Mackenzie • Bob Mackie • Patti MacLeod • Dave Madden • Patty Maloney • Robert Mandan • Irene Mandrell • Stephen Manley • Randolph Mantooth • Rose Marie • Monte Markham • Peter Marshall • Dick Martin • Jared Martin • Pamela Sue Martin • Ross Martin • Nobu McCarthy • Rue McClanahan • Marilyn McCoo • Kent McCord • Patty McCormack • Maureen McCormick • Pat McCormick • Mary McDonough • Roddy McDowall • Darren McGaven • Nancy McKeon • John McIntire • Allyn An McLerie • Kristy McNichol • Audrey Meadows • Anne Meara • John Meehan • Eddie Mekka • Gabriel Melgar • Heather Menzies • Lee Meriwether • Ethel Merman • Vera Miles • Ray Milland • Ann Miller • Denise Miller • Donna Mills • Hayley Mills • Juliet Mills • Sir John Mills • Keith Mitchell • Mary Ann Mobley • Al Molinaro • Kelly Monteith • Belinda J. Montgomery • Lynne Moody • Melba Moore • Terry Moore • Erin Moran • Cindy Morgan • Debbi Morgan • Dennis Morgan • Harry Morgan • Henry Morgan • Jaye P. Morgan • Pat Morita • Greg Morris • Karen Morrow • Donny Most • Diana Muldaur • Richard Mulligan • Robert Mulligan • Ben Murphy • Jim Nabors • Joe Namath • Mildred Natwick • Melinda Naud • Connie Needham • Barry Nelson • David Nelson • Harriet Nelson • Rick Nelson • Lois Nettleton • Julie Newmar • Denise Nicholas • Denise Nicholas-Hill • Leslie Nielson • James Noble • Trisha Noble • Jeannette Nolan • Kathleen Nolan • Christopher Norris • Judy Norton-Taylor • Shelly Novack • Louis Nye • Hugh O'Brian • Donald O'Connor • Lani O'Grady • Randi Oakes • Susan Oliver • Donny Osmond • Jimmy Osmond • Lawanda Page • Janis Paige • Ron Palillio • Betsy Palmer • Eleanor Parker • Bert Parks • Catherine Parks • Minnie Pearl • Meeno Peluce • Donna Pescow • Joanna Petter • Jo Ann Pflug • Mackenzie Phillips • Michelle Phillips • Mark Pinter • Eve Plumb • The Pointer Sisters • Don Porter • Markie Post • Tom Poston • Jane Powell • Randall Powell • Joan Prather • Vincent Price • Juliet Prowse • Charlotte Rae • Dacko Rambo • Gene Rayburn • Martha Raye • Robert Rayes • Helen Reddy • Robert Reed • Tracy Reed • Della Reese • Charles Nelson Reilly • Alejandro Rey • Debbie Reynolds • Barbara Rhoades • Adam Rich • Susan Richardson • John Ritter • Doris Roberts • Pernell Roberts • Tanya Roberts • Tony Roberts • Dale Robertson • John Mark Robinson • Ginger Rogers • Marion Ross • Dan Rowan • Misty Rowe • Richard Roundtree • John Rubinstein • Barbara Rush • Nipsey Russell • Soupy Sales • Jennifer Salt • Isabel Sanford • Dean Santro • Dick Sargent • Brad Savage • Ronnie Scribner • Natalie Schafer • Ronnie Schell • Avery Schreiber • Debralee Scott • Martha Scott • Mark Serra • Jennifer Shaw • Dick Shawn • Mark Shera • Bobby Sherman • Bobby Short • Stephen Shortridge • Sonny Shrover • Sylvia Sidney • Charles Siebeert • Phil Silvers • Walker Slezak • Jaclyn Smith • Rex Smith • Shelley Smith • Tom Smothers • Jack Somack • Brett Somers • Suzanne Somers • Elke Sommer • Laurette Spang • Camilla Spary • Jill St. John • Robert Stack • Jim Stafford • Bernadette Stanis • Jim Stafford • Lajaine Stephens • Skip Stephenson • Connie Stevens • Craig Stevens • Marti Stevens • Mclean Stevenson • Trish Stewart • Jerry Stiller • Larry Storch • Susan Strasper • WK Stratton • Barry Sullivan • Shauna Sullivan • Susan Sullivan • Loretta Swit • Brenda Sykes • Robert Symonds • Jeff Tambor • Vic Tayback • Leigh Taylor-Young • Toni Tennille • Lauren Tewes • Mark Thomas • Kevin Tighe • Charlene Tilton • Johnny Timko • Michele Tobin • Berlinda Tolbert • Fred Travelana • Ellen Travolta • Michael Tucci • Forrest Tucker • Tanya Tucker • Leslie Uggams • Bob Urich • Robert Urich • Karen Valentine • Bobby Van • Joan Van Ark • Barry Van Dyke • Dick Van Patten • Vincent Van Patton • Gloria Vanderbilt • Robert Vau • Ben Vereen • Abe Vigoda • The Village People • Sal Viscuso • Lyle Waggoner • Marcia Wallace • Jimmie Walker • Nancy Walker • Jessica Walter • Carlene Watkins • Vernee Watson • Kristina Wayborn • Patrick Wayne • Dawn Wells • Judy West • Jill Whelan • Andjesse White • Betty White • Larry Wilcox • Fred Willard • Anson Williams • Paul Williams • Desmond Wilson • Flip Wilson • William Windom • Edward Winter • Jane Withers • Alex Woddard • Jo Anne Worley • Jane Wyatt • Jane Wyman • Dana Wynter • Alan Young • Michael Young • Jonny Yune • Michael Zaslow • Stephanie Zimbalist

THE PLAIN, THE PLAIN!
NO, THE GLAZED, THE GLAZED!

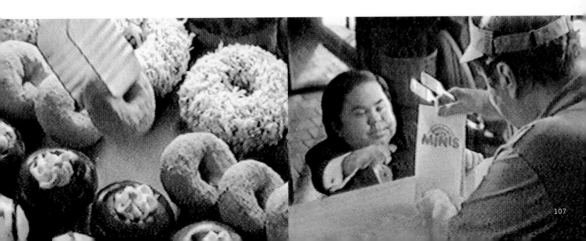

buddy

♂

doug

ted

felix

bobby

kevin

sam

bridget loves bernie

fred

john

charles

luke

oscar

barney

sam

ed

trixie

gloria

ethel

alice

pam

olivia

blanche

betty

joanie loves chachi

julie

winnie

♀

laura

pickles

georgette

diane

caroline

buddy loves pickles (the dick van dyke show) • doug loves julie (days of our lives) • ted loves georgette (the mary tyler moore show) • felix loved gloria (the odd couple) • bobby loves pam (dallas) • kevin loves winnie (the wonder years) • sam loves diane (cheers) • fred loves ethel (i love lucy) • john loves olivia (the waltons) • charles loves caroline (little house on the prairie) • luke loves laura (general hospital) • oscar loved blanche (the odd couple) • barney loves betty (the flintstones) • sam loves alice (the brady bunch) • ed loves trixie (the honeymooners)

Diff'rent Strokes

The Facts of Life

Webster

Gimme a Break

Small Wonder

Punky Brewster

Blossom

My Two Dads

Full House

111

Manly, yes. But I like it, too!

WOULDN'T YOU LIKE TO BE A PEPPER, TOO?

You're soaking in it!

WHEN YOU'RE OUT OF SCHLITZ, YOU'RE OUT OF BEER!

Please, don't squeeze the Charmin!

Leggo my Eggo!

I CAN BRING HOME THE BACON, FRY IT UP IN A PAN...

Pass the cookies and pass the cow. Pillsbury cookies and cow, WOW!

Towers . Masterpiece Theatre . Upstairs, Downstairs . Flambards . Absolutely Fabulous . The Young Ones . Dr. Who . Monty Python . Benny Hill . Fawlty

Mr. Microphone

Zamfir, master of the pan flute

ch-ch-ch-**chia!**

GLH

Ginsu Knives

It slices, it dices!

Turn ordinary bottles into attractive glasses!

Ronco

Seal-A-Meal

clap on, clap off!

Popeil's Pocket Fisherman

Thigh Master

I've **fallen** and I can't get up!

Flowbee

John Candy ○ **Bob and Doug McKenzie**

○ **Joe Flaherty** ○ "The Great White North" ○

Eugene Levy ○ Andrea Martin ○ **Rick Moranis**

○ **Edith Prickley** ○ Catherine O'Hara ○

Tex and Edna Boil's Organ Emporium

○ Dave Thomas ○ **Guy Caballero**

○ "The Sammy Maudlin Show" ○

"Days of the Week" ○ "The Cruising

Gourmet" ○ "The Fracases,

America's Nastiest Couple"

○ **Billy Sol Hurok**

& Big Jim McBob

○ **Count Floyd** ○ "Scaaary!"

Things Go Better with Coke **It's the Real Thing** I'd Like to Buy the World a Coke
Coke Adds Life Coke Is It Red, White and You Can't Beat the Feeling

Catch the wave. **Coke**

Think Young! Come Alive! You're in the Pepsi Generation! Pepsi Pours It On! You've Got a Lot to Live, Pepsi's Got a Lot to Give Join the Pepsi People, Feelin' Free! Have a Pepsi Day! Take the Pepsi Challenge!

The Newlywed Game

BERT CONVY

DICK CLARK

Name That Tune

PEGGY CASS

Tattletales

"Will the real _____

please stand up."

Match Game

Split Second

ALAN LUDDEN

KITTY CARLISLE

It's Your Bet

FAMILY FEUD

The Wizard of Odds

The Dating Game

WINK MARTINDALE

Three on a Match

BOB EUBANKS

Truth or Consequences

Joker's Wild

"I'LL TAKE CHARLEY WEAVER TO BLOCK."

"Enter and sign in, please.

Password

Jeopardy!

CAROL MERRILL

Baffle

GENE RAYBURN

BILL CULLEN

Concentration

Gambit

Dealer's Choice

PETER MARSHALL

[A MARK GOODSON–BILL TODMAN PRODUCTION]

Beat the Clock

Call My Bluff

CHARLES NELSON-REILLY

PAUL LYNDE

THE $100,000 PYRAMID

Winning Streak

High Rollers

BOB BARKER

127

People Do The Craziest Things

The Gong Show

The $1.98 Beauty Contest

Kids Are People, Too

That's Incredible!

The Art Linkletter Show

Real People

America's Funniest Home Videos

The Guinness Book of World Records

Totally Hidden Video

This Is Your Life

Queen for a Day

Smile
YOU'RE ON
Candid Camera!

STILL THE ONE
THE NETWORK OF THE NEW
THE BEST IS RIGHT HERE ON CBS
COME AND SEE!
THIS IS THE PLACE TO BE
NBCABCCBS

PUT A TIC TAC IN YOUR MOUTH AND GET A BANG OUT OF LIFE...MM! MM! GOOD! MM! MM! GOOD! THAT'S WHAT CAMPBELL'S SOUPS ARE, MM! MM! GOOD!...I AM STUCK ON BAND-AID AND BAND-AID'S STUCK ON ME!...SOMETIMES YOU FEEL LIKE A NUT, SOMETIMES YOU DON'T...

☞ **Booker**

The Cosby Show ☞

☞ **Melrose Place** ☞

☞ **The Joey Bishop Show**

☞ **The Brady Brides**

132

Fish

Burke's Law

Hill Street Blues

Sanford

The Sanford Arms

 Enos

133

Apple's Way

Eight Is Enough

Family

The Family Holvak

The Fitzpatricks

Little House On The Prairie

Mulligan's Stew

The New Land

Shirley

PLOP PLOP

PLOP

FIZZ

FIZZ

(OH WHAT A RELIEF IT IS!)

TUMS FOR THE TUMMY

I can't believe I ate the whole thing... You ate it Ralph, you ate it...

How do you spell relief?

indiGESTion!

Didn't find your
fondest memory in
Do You Remember TV?
Fax it to us for
Volume Three at
(212) 873-7223.
Or E-mail us your suggestions.
Reach us online at
TakeUBack@aol.com or at
www.doyouremember.com